FOIL

FOR CAMPFIRES & GRILLS

PACKS

What's a foil pack?

It's a great way to cook on a campfire or grill without dirtying dishes! Assemble food on some heavy-duty foil and wrap it up to make an airtight pack. Then toss the pack on some hot coals or a grill grate and let it cook. Just open the pack and dig in.

Safety Reminders

Foil packs get hot. Use long tongs and oven mitts to pick them up and move them. Support heavy packs underneath. Steam forms inside the packs during cooking and it's very hot, so always open them slowly to let the steam escape..

*Actual cooking times are affected by the heat of your fire, the weather, and the thickness of your food. **Use the times listed in these recipes as estimates and then check your packs often as you cook.***

Printed in China

Distributed By:

507 Industrial Street
Waverly, IA 50677

ISBN-13: 978-1-56383-524-7
Item #2913

Foil Pack Basics

- Make single-serving packs for individual meals or create family-style packs to share.

- Cut a large piece of heavy-duty foil for each pack. One layer is sturdy enough for small packs, but double it for large ones.

- To prevent sticking, spritz foil with cooking spray, or for sweet or cheesy recipes, line the foil with parchment paper.

- Ingredients like onions, water, ice cubes, soups, or sauces help produce steam inside the pack to cook food and keep it moist.

- Check foil packs often during cooking to monitor doneness. Move them frequently to cook evenly and avoid burn spots.

Cooking on a Campfire

- Let firewood burn down until you can break off hot glowing coals for cooking. Spread them out and set the foil packs right on top. More coals = higher heat.

- For indirect or low heat, push the coals aside and arrange hot coals around the packs.

- Add more coals, move them around, or replenish as needed during cooking for even heat.

Cooking on a Grill

- Preheat the grill before starting, and cook with the lid closed.

- Use the temperature gauge on a gas grill to regulate the heat *(about 300° for low, 350° for medium, and 400° or more for high heat).*

- If using charcoal briquettes, estimate the temperature by carefully holding your hand above the glowing coals. *(It's about 350° if you can hold your hand there for 3-4 seconds.)*

- For indirect heat, fire up one side of the grill and place foil packs on the other side so food isn't directly over the heat.

Wrap It Up!

The secret to successful foil pack cooking? A leak-proof pouch that locks in moisture and flavor. Place your food in the center of a large piece of foil and then wrap it up in one of two ways:

1 Make a **TENT PACK** to cook vegetables, fruits, the Classic Hobo Dinner, and other combination packs that need lots of steam but less browning.

2 Make a **FLAT PACK** to cook meat, fish, and other foods that need less steam and more browning.

Classic Hobo Dinner

layer food in the center

heavy-duty aluminum foil (don't skimp!)

carrots (celery, corn & green beans are good too)

butter (or add extra flavor with a little creamed soup or barbeque sauce)

potatoes

salt & pepper (& other favorite seasonings)

ground beef patty (or try other meat)

onion (for flavor & moisture)

3 Easy Steps

1 For both tent packs and flat packs, bring foil edges together on top. Fold over and crease well.

2 Then roll the top edge down a couple of times and pinch together tightly.

For tent packs, leave some space above food for air to circulate.

For flat packs press that foil nice and flat against the food.

3 Lastly, roll up each end to seal both types of packs.

To Cook

Set the hobo pack on hot coals or medium-high heat on a grill for 25 to 30 minutes, until meat is done and vegetables are tender. Rotate the pack several times during cooking. Open carefully and dig in!

Cabbage Wedges

Wash and quarter a head of cabbage. Brush each wedge with 2 T. soft butter and sprinkle with salt, pepper, garlic salt, and grated Parmesan cheese to taste. Wrap 1 bacon strip around each wedge and then wrap food with sprayed foil to make four tent packs. Cook as directed, until cabbage is tender and bacon is done. **Serves 4**

To grill, set foil packs on the grate over medium-low heat and cook 25 to 30 minutes, turning once.

At the campfire, set foil packs on a few hot coals surrounded by more heat. Cook 25 to 35 minutes, rotating and flipping packs over once or twice. Set some hot coals on top of packs for the last 5 to 10 minutes to brown the bacon.

Creamy Cheese Dip

Set a 5½" to 6" disposable foil pie pan *(12 oz. capacity)* on a large piece of foil *(or omit pan and just use two layers of heavy-duty foil)*. Spoon 1 (8 oz.) tub chive & onion or jalapeño cream cheese spread into the pan and pour ¾ C. salsa over it. Top with 1 small diced tomato and 2 sliced green onions. Wrap foil around the pan in a tent pack, sealing well. Cook as directed until warm and melty. *(Shorten the cooking time if making dip without the pan.)* Serve with tortilla or bagel chips, raw vegetables, crackers, or breadsticks. **Serves 4-6**

To grill, set foil pack on the grate over medium heat and cook about 20 minutes.

At the campfire, set foil pack on hot coals and cook 15 to 25 minutes.

Hot Parmesan Bread

6 T. butter, softened

⅓ C. grated Parmesan cheese

Garlic powder & Italian seasoning to taste

1 loaf French bread, cut into 1" thick slices

Directions

In a small bowl, mix butter and cheese; stir in seasonings. Spread the butter mixture over one side of each bread slice. Reassemble slices into a loaf and wrap snugly in foil. Cook as directed. **Serves 8-12**

Cooking Methods

Set foil pack on the grill's top shelf over medium heat or directly on the grate over medium-low heat. Cover grill and cook 8 to 12 minutes or until hot, flipping pack over partway through cooking time.

Set foil pack on warm coals surrounded by more heat. Cook 12 to 14 minutes or until hot, rotating and flipping pack over partway through cooking time.

Want it cheesier? Try slicing a loaf of ciabatta or focaccia bread in half horizontally and then spread both halves with the butter mixture; add a layer of cheese (like cheddar, Swiss, Brie, or provolone) and reassemble the loaf. Wrap in foil and cook as directed.

Lasagna over a fire? Why not! These luscious layers will have you saying, "Magnifico!"

Grilled Lasagna

1 lb. ground sausage

1 C. chopped mushrooms

½ C. chopped onion

1 lb. fresh mozzarella cheese, thinly sliced

½ C. shredded Parmesan cheese, plus more for serving

½ tsp. red pepper flakes

1 tsp. minced garlic

Salt & pepper to taste

Olive oil

3 tomatoes, thinly sliced, plus more for serving

12 no-boil lasagna noodles, divided

½ (6 oz.) pkg. baby spinach

Fresh basil

Directions

Cook sausage, mushrooms, and onion in a skillet; let cool. In a bowl, combine both cheeses and all seasonings; drizzle with 2 tablespoons oil and toss well. Sprinkle tomatoes with salt and pepper.

Stack two long pieces of foil together and drizzle oil down the center of top piece. Set one noodle lengthwise on foil and sprinkle evenly with 1 tablespoon water. Repeat the process for three more foil packs. Use half each of the spinach, sausage mixture, tomatoes, and cheese mixture to make one layer of each ingredient on the noodles. Top each with a second noodle and sprinkle with 1 tablespoon water. Repeat layers with remaining filling ingredients. Set a third noodle on each stack; coat with 1 tablespoon water and drizzle with oil. Wrap foil around food to make four flat packs and cook as directed. Before serving, top with more sliced tomatoes, Parmesan cheese, and some snipped basil. **Serves 4-8**

Cooking Methods

Set foil packs on the grate over indirect medium heat and cover grill. Cook 10 minutes; flip packs over and cook about 10 minutes more. Let rest 5 minutes before opening.

Set foil packs on a few hot coals surrounded by more heat. Cook 10 to 15 minutes. Flip packs over and cook 10 to 15 minutes more. Let rest 5 minutes before opening.

Corn on the Cob

4 ears of sweet corn, shucked

¼ C. butter, sliced (or olive oil)

Salt & pepper

Parmesan cheese, optional

Fresh rosemary to taste

8 ice cubes

Directions

Place two ears of corn on each large sheet of sprayed foil. Set a few butter slices on top of each ear. Sprinkle with salt, pepper, and Parmesan cheese, if desired. Add a few rosemary sprigs. Set two ice cubes beside each ear of corn and wrap foil around corn to make two tent packs. Cook as directed. **Serves 4**

Cooking Methods

Set foil packs on the grate over medium heat and cover grill. Cook 20 minutes or until tender and hot.

Set foil packs on medium-hot coals and cook 20 minutes or until tender and hot.

You can put all the ears in one big pack, if you prefer, but cook it a little longer.

Glazed Pork Chop Packs

2 boneless pork chops

⅔ C. peach or apricot preserves

2 T. soy sauce

Garlic powder, salt & pepper to taste

1 (16 oz.) bag frozen stir-fry vegetables, thawed

Directions

Place each pork chop on a large piece of foil. In a bowl, stir together the preserves, soy sauce, and seasonings. Spread ¼ of the peach mixture over each chop. Arrange half the vegetables over and around each chop. Pour the remaining peach mixture evenly over both packs. Wrap foil around food to make two tent packs and cook as directed. **Serves 2**

Cooking Methods

Set foil packs on the grate over medium heat and cover grill. Cook 20 minutes or until vegetables are tender and meat is done *(internal temperature of meat should reach 145°)*. Let rest 5 minutes.

Set foil packs on medium-hot coals and cook 20 minutes or until vegetables are tender and meat is done *(internal temperature of meat should reach 145°)*. Let rest 5 minutes.

We used ribeye chops and mandarin-style veggies.

Apple Tortilla Strudel

For each strudel, set 1 (10") flour tortilla on a large piece of sprayed foil. Arrange 1½ T. sliced butter across the center and layer with ½ C. diced apple, 1 T. brown sugar, some cinnamon, and 2 T. each chopped pecans and granola cereal. *(Try other combos like peanut butter, diced apple, brown sugar, peanuts, and chocolate chips.)* Roll up the tortilla burrito-style, folding ends in to keep filling inside. Place seam side down on foil and wrap to make a flat pack. Cook as directed until apples are tender. **Each pack serves 1-2**

To grill, set foil pack(s) on the grate over medium heat and cover grill. Cook 10 to 15 minutes, flipping over once.

At the campfire, set foil pack(s) on medium coals and cook 10 to 20 minutes, flipping over once.

French Bread Dip

Cut the top off a French bread loaf; remove the center to leave a ½"-thick shell. Cube removed bread and trim crust piece to make a "lid." Mix 1 (8 oz.) pkg. softened cream cheese, 2 C. sour cream, 2 C. shredded cheddar cheese, ½ C. diced ham, 2 chopped green onions, 1 tsp. Worcestershire sauce, and ¼ tsp. hot sauce. Season with salt and pepper. Fill shell with dip and top with lid; wrap in parchment paper-lined foil. Cook as directed and serve with bread cubes or crackers. **Serves 12**

To grill, set foil pack on the grate over indirect medium heat and cover grill. Cook about 1 hour or until hot.

At the campfire, set foil pack on a few warm coals surrounded by more heat. Cook about 1 hour or until hot, rotating pack several times.

Summer Veggies

1 zucchini, diced

1 yellow summer squash, diced

4 fresh mushrooms, sliced

2 mini bell peppers, any color, diced

½ to 1 jalapeño pepper, seeded & finely diced

2 tsp. olive oil

1½ C. cooked quinoa

1 to 2 tsp. garlic powder

Salt & pepper to taste

Directions

In a large bowl, combine zucchini, squash, mushrooms, bell peppers, and jalapeño. Drizzle with oil and stir until coated. Place the cooked quinoa in the center of a large piece of sprayed foil. Spoon the vegetables on top and sprinkle evenly with seasonings. Wrap foil around the food in a tent pack and cook as directed. **Serves 4**

Cooking Methods

Set foil pack on the grate over medium heat and cover grill. Cook about 5 minutes. Flip pack over and cook 5 to 10 minutes more or until vegetables are tender.

Set foil pack on hot coals and cook 5 to 10 minutes. Flip pack over and cook 5 to 10 minutes more or until vegetables are tender.

Cajun Jambalaya

1 lb. raw medium shrimp, peeled & cleaned

6 to 8 oz. Andouille pork sausage, thinly sliced

1 (14.5 oz.) can diced tomatoes with garlic & olive oil

2 tsp. dried minced onion

4 C. cooked rice

1 green bell pepper, cored & diced

3 to 4 tsp. Cajun seasoning

1 tsp. hot pepper sauce

Directions

In a large bowl, toss together the shrimp, sausage, tomatoes, onion, cooked rice, bell pepper, Cajun seasoning, and pepper sauce. Divide the mixture among four large pieces of sprayed foil. Wrap foil around food to make four tent packs, sealing well. Cook as directed. **Serves 4**

Cooking Methods

Set foil packs on the grate over medium-high heat and cover grill. Cook 8 to 10 minutes or until shrimp are pink and everything is heated through.

Set foil packs on hot coals and cook 10 to 15 minutes, rotating once, until shrimp are pink and everything is heated through.

Transfer any leftovers to an airtight container. Spicy and acidic foods can cause foil to become pitted after an extended time.

Breakfast Subs

6 (6") bolillo or hero rolls or
sourdough baguettes

10 eggs

⅔ C. half & half

8 bacon strips, cooked
& crumbled

1½ C. shredded
cheddar cheese

4 green onions, sliced

Salt & pepper to taste

Directions

Cut a deep "V" through the top of each roll, stopping ½" from the bottom. Pull out some bread from the center, leaving ½"-thick shells *("boats")*. Set each boat in the center of a large piece of sprayed foil.

In a bowl, whisk together the eggs and half & half. Stir in bacon, cheese, onions, salt, and pepper. Divide mixture evenly among bread boats. Wrap foil around food to make six flat packs. Cook as directed. **Serves 6**

Cooking Methods

Set foil packs on the grate over medium heat and cover grill. Cook 15 to 20 minutes or until puffed and set in the center. Let rest 5 minutes before serving.

Set foil packs on a few hot coals surrounded by more heat. Cook 15 to 25 minutes, rotating once or twice, until puffed and set in the center. Let rest 5 minutes before serving.

Taco-Tater Meal

1 lb. lean ground beef
   or turkey

2 T. taco seasoning

¼ C. milk

3 C. frozen diced hash
   browns, thawed

Salt & pepper to taste

1 C. cheese salsa dip

Tomato salsa

Directions

In a bowl, combine meat, taco seasoning, and milk; mix well. Lightly shape into four even patties. Place each patty in the center of a large piece of sprayed foil. Spread an equal amount of hash browns over each meat patty and sprinkle with salt and pepper. Spoon ¼ cup cheese dip over each serving. Wrap foil around food to make four tent packs. Cook as directed.
Serves 4

Cooking Methods

Set foil packs on the grate over medium heat and cover grill. Cook 15 to 20 minutes or until meat is done, rotating packs once during cooking.

Set foil packs on hot coals and cook 20 to 25 minutes or until meat is done, rotating packs partway through cooking time.

Bacon-Onion Potatoes

Cook and crumble 8 bacon strips. Remove skins and stem ends from 1½ C. frozen (thawed) pearl onions. Halve 2 lbs. fingerling potatoes. Combine onions and potatoes in a bowl and toss with ¼ C. olive oil, 1 T. minced garlic, and 1 tsp. dried thyme; season with salt and pepper. Divide mixture among four large pieces of spayed foil and sprinkle each with crumbled bacon and 1 T. Parmesan cheese. Wrap foil around food to make four tent packs. Cook as directed until potatoes are tender. **Serves 4**

To grill, set foil packs on the grate over medium heat and cover grill. Cook 30 to 35 minutes, flipping over once.

At the campfire, set foil packs on hot coals and cook 30 to 35 minutes, flipping over twice.

Buffalo Chicken Bread

Slice a loaf of Vienna bread in half crosswise and lengthwise. Mix 2 T. buffalo wing sauce, ¼ C. blue cheese dressing, and ½ C. ranch dressing. Reserve ¼ C. sauce mixture; spread remainder on bread. Toss 1½ C. cooked chicken with reserved sauce and arrange evenly on bread. Top each piece with ¼ C. each shredded cheddar and Monterey Jack, 2 T. shredded Parmesan, and 1 T. crumbled blue cheese; press lightly. Wrap in parchment paper-lined foil to make four flat packs. Cook as directed until hot and melty. **Serves 4**

To grill, set foil packs on the grate over indirect medium heat and cover grill. Cook 25 to 30 minutes, rotating once.

At the campfire, set foil packs on warm coals surrounded by more heat. Cook 10 to 20 minutes, rotating once.

Warm pita pockets filled with chunks of tender salmon and the trimmings – Greek perfection!

Salmon Pitas

1 (6 oz.) carton plain Greek yogurt

1 T. snipped fresh basil

¾ to 1 tsp. dried dill weed

4 (4 oz.) frozen salmon fillets, thawed

1 small red or yellow onion, thinly sliced

1 T. olive oil, divided

Salt & pepper to taste

4 thin lemon slices, divided

6 pita bread pockets

Chopped romaine lettuce

1 C. halved grape tomatoes

Directions

In a small bowl, mix yogurt, basil, and dill weed; cover and chill until serving time.

Pat fillets dry with paper towels. Place half the onion in the center of a large piece of sprayed foil and arrange two salmon pieces on top. Drizzle with 1½ teaspoons oil and sprinkle with salt and pepper. Top with two lemon slices and wrap foil around food in a tent pack. Repeat to make a second foil pack. Stack pita pockets together and wrap tightly in another piece of foil. Cook as directed. **Makes 6 pitas**

Cooking Methods

Set salmon foil packs on the grate over medium-high heat and cover grill. Cook 10 to 12 minutes or until fish begins to flake with a fork. Warm the pita foil pack on the grate during the last 5 minutes of cooking time, turning once.

Set salmon foil packs on a few hot coals and cook 10 to 12 minutes or until fish begins to flake with a fork. Heat the pita foil pack on warm coals during the last 5 minutes of cooking time, turning once.

To Assemble & Serve

Open salmon packs and discard lemon slices. With a fork, pull salmon apart in chunks. Place some lettuce, salmon with onion, and tomatoes in each warm pita and serve with the chilled yogurt mixture.

Stuffed peppers in a foil pack? It was meant to be... just look at that cheese. It's melted heaven!

Philly-Stuffed Peppers

- 2 T. butter
- 2 T. olive oil
- 1 sweet onion, sliced in rings
- 6 oz. sliced baby bella mushrooms
- 1 T. minced garlic
- Salt & pepper to taste
- ½ lb. deli sliced roast beef
- 2 green bell peppers
- 8 slices provolone cheese, divided

Directions

In a skillet over medium heat, combine butter and oil; when hot, add onion, mushrooms, garlic, salt, and pepper. Sauté over low heat until onions and mushrooms are soft and caramelized, about 20 minutes. Add the beef and cook 10 minutes more.

Slice bell peppers in half lengthwise; remove stems, seeds, and white ribs. Line each pepper "shell" with a slice of cheese. Fill each shell generously with the meat mixture and top with another slice of cheese. Line four large pieces of foil with parchment paper. Wrap parchment-lined foil snugly around each stuffed pepper to make four flat packs. Cook as directed.
Serves 4

Cooking Methods

 Set foil packs on the grate over medium heat and cover grill. Cook 15 to 20 minutes or until peppers are tender and cheese is melted

 Set foil packs on hot coals and cook 15 to 20 minutes or until peppers are tender and cheese is melted. Rotate the packs once or twice during cooking.

For convenience, prep the meat mixture ahead of time and refrigerate it in an airtight container until ready to use. Many foil packs can be prepped, assembled, and chilled until needed.

Hawaiian Ham Packs

1 large sweet potato, peeled & diced

½ lb. cubed ham

1 red bell pepper, cored & sliced in rings

4 canned pineapple slices, drained

2 T. butter

2 T. brown sugar

Red pepper flakes to taste

Directions

Divide sweet potato pieces among two large pieces of sprayed foil. Layer the ham and bell pepper rings evenly over potatoes. Arrange two pineapple rings on each pack and top each with half the butter and half the brown sugar. Sprinkle with pepper flakes. Wrap foil around food to make two tent packs and cook as directed. **Serves 2**

Cooking Methods

Set foil packs on the grate over medium-high heat and cover grill. Cook about 20 minutes or until potatoes are tender, flipping packs over during the last 5 minutes to lightly brown the pineapple.

Set foil packs on hot coals and cook about 20 minutes, rotating packs once, until potatoes are tender. Flip packs over during the last 5 minutes to lightly brown the pineapple.

Add a few mini marshmallows on top as soon as your packs come off the fire. Sweet!

An all-in-one delicious foil meal experience. Add any other veggies you want to change it up a bit.

BBQ Meatball Dinner

1 C. chopped onion

5 or 6 medium red potatoes, scrubbed & quartered

3 carrots, peeled & sliced in rounds

1 C. fresh sliced mushrooms

1 lb. lean ground beef

1 T. Worcestershire sauce

1 tsp. minced garlic

½ C. cooked rice

Barbecue sauce

¼ C. butter, softened

2 to 3 tsp. fresh rosemary (or ¾ tsp. dried)

Salt & pepper to taste

Directions

Line three or four large pieces of foil with parchment paper. Divide the onion, potatoes, carrots, and mushrooms evenly among foil pieces and set aside.

In a large bowl, combine beef, Worcestershire sauce, garlic, and cooked rice; mix well with your hands. Lightly shape the mixture into 10 to 12 (1½") meatballs. Place three or four meatballs on the vegetables in each pack and drizzle with 2 tablespoons barbecue sauce.

In a small bowl, mix the butter and rosemary; add a few dollops to each pack. Season with salt and pepper and wrap the packs tent-style. Cook as directed. **Serves 3-4**

Cooking Methods

Set foil packs on the grate over indirect high heat and cover grill. Cook about 30 minutes or until meat is done and vegetables are tender.

Set foil packs on a few hot coals surrounded by more heat. Cook about 30 minutes or until meat is done and vegetables are tender. Rotate packs several times during cooking and place several hot coals on top of each pack during the last 10 minutes.

> *Heavy-duty foil that's 18" wide works well for packs like these.*

Southern Succotash

On a large double thickness of sprayed foil, layer 1 (16 oz.) bag frozen lima beans, 2 C. frozen corn kernels, and 1 diced red bell pepper. Sprinkle with 1 tsp. dried thyme; season with salt and pepper. Add 2 T. butter and wrap foil around vegetables to make one tent pack. Cook as directed, adding ¼ C. heavy cream halfway through cooking time. **Serves 8-10**

To grill, set foil pack on the grate over medium-high heat and cook 15 minutes. Open the pack and stir in cream; reseal foil and cook 15 to 20 minutes more.

At the campfire, set foil pack on hot coals and cook 15 minutes. Remove from heat, open pack, and stir in cream; reseal foil and return to coals. Cook 15 to 20 minutes more.

Tater Tot Bake

Divide 1 (32 oz.) bag frozen tater tots among two large pieces of sprayed foil. Layer each pack evenly with ½ C. chopped onion, ½ (4 oz.) can drained mushrooms, ½ (4 oz.) jar drained pimentos, and ¼ C. sliced butter. Wrap foil around food to make two flat packs and cook as directed until onion is tender and everything is hot. Mash up the mixture before serving, if desired. **Serves 4**

To grill, set foil packs on the grate over medium heat and cover grill. Cook 20 to 30 minutes.

At the campfire, set foil packs over medium coals and cook 20 to 30 minutes.

Southwestern Chicken

1 (15 oz.) can black beans, drained & rinsed

2 C. frozen whole kernel corn

1 (10 oz.) can diced tomatoes & green chiles, drained

½ tsp. ground cumin

4 boneless, skinless chicken breast halves

½ C. shredded Mexican cheese blend

Salsa for serving

Directions

In a bowl, stir together beans, corn, tomatoes, and cumin. Place each piece of chicken in the center of a large piece of sprayed foil. Spoon about 1 cup bean mixture over the chicken in each pack, dividing it evenly. Wrap foil around food to make four tent packs and cook as directed. Serve with salsa. **Serves 4**

Cooking Methods

Set foil packs on the grate over medium-high heat and cover grill. Cook 15 to 20 minutes or until chicken is done *(internal temperature should reach 165°)*. Open the packs and sprinkle with cheese. Reseal and let rest until cheese melts, about 2 minutes.

Set foil packs on hot coals and cook 15 to 20 minutes or until chicken is done *(internal temperature should reach 165°)*. Rotate packs partway through cooking time. Open the packs and sprinkle with cheese. Reseal and let rest until cheese melts, about 2 minutes.

Pizza-Stuffed Zucchini

2 medium zucchini

Olive oil

½ lb. ground turkey or sausage

1 tsp. dried oregano

1 tsp. dried basil

Salt & pepper to taste

1½ C. cheese & garlic pasta sauce (or other spaghetti sauce)

¾ C. shredded mozzarella cheese

Directions

Cut each zucchini in half horizontally and scoop out the center to make "boats" about ½" thick. Brush edges with oil and set aside.

In a saucepan, heat 1 tablespoon oil. Add turkey, herbs, and seasonings; brown meat until crumbly. Drain off excess fat and stir in sauce; cook until heated through. Divide the turkey mixture evenly among zucchini boats and sprinkle with cheese; press lightly. Wrap each boat in parchment paper-lined foil to make four tent packs. Cook as directed. **Serves 4**

Cooking Methods

 Set foil packs on the grate over medium heat and cover grill. Cook about 15 minutes or until tender.

 Set foil packs on a few hot coals surrounded by more heat. Cook 15 to 20 minutes or until tender. Rotate packs once during cooking.

A melon baller works well to scoop out the zucchini.

Easy Breakfast Hash

Seasoned salt

¼ C. butter, sliced, divided

6 eggs

1 (28 to 30 oz.) bag shredded hash browns

1 medium onion, chopped

½ lb. cubed ham or chopped Canadian bacon

1½ to 2 C. shredded smoked Swiss & cheddar cheese

Garlic powder & pepper to taste

Directions

Stack two long pieces of foil together and spray top piece with cooking spray. Sprinkle with seasoned salt and add half the butter slices; bend foil edges up slightly.

Whisk eggs in a bowl. Cut open the bag of hash browns at the top and set it upright. Add eggs, onion, ham, and cheese to bag; squeeze bag until mixed. Spread mixture on foil. Sprinkle with seasonings and top with remaining butter slices. Place another double layer of sprayed foil on top and seal all edges together to make one large flat pack. Cook as directed. **Serves 8**

Cooking Methods

 Set foil pack on the grate over medium heat and cook 30 to 40 minutes until eggs are cooked and potatoes are lightly browned. Flip pack over several times during cooking.

 Set foil pack on a few hot coals surrounded by more heat. Cook 30 to 40 minutes, rotating pack and flipping over several times, until eggs are cooked and everything is hot. Toward the end of cooking time, set a few hot coals on top of pack to promote browning.

Ranch Chicken Dinner

2 boneless, skinless chicken breast halves

¼ tsp. Montreal Chicken Seasoning, divided

¼ C. ranch salad dressing, divided

2 T. water

2 C. quartered small red potatoes

2 carrots, peeled & sliced into sticks

2 C. fresh green beans, trimmed

2 T. shredded Parmesan cheese, divided

Directions

Set each chicken breast half on a large piece of sprayed foil. Sprinkle each chicken piece with ⅛ teaspoon Montreal seasoning and drizzle with 1 tablespoon dressing. In a large bowl, mix remaining 2 tablespoons dressing with water. Add potatoes, carrots, and green beans; stir until well coated. Divide vegetables evenly among chicken pieces and pour any remaining liquid around the edges. Sprinkle each with 1 tablespoon cheese. Wrap foil around food to make two tent packs and cook as directed. **Serves 2**

Cooking Methods

 Set foil packs on the grate over medium heat and cover grill. Cook 20 to 25 minutes or until vegetables are crisp-tender and chicken is done *(internal temperature should reach 165°)*.

 Set foil packs on medium coals and cook 25 to 30 minutes or until vegetables are crisp-tender and chicken is done *(internal temperature should reach 165°)*.

Lemon-Parm Broccoli

FAMILY STYLE PACK

Spread 1 (10.8 oz.) bag frozen, partially thawed broccoli on a double layer of sprayed foil *("steamable" broccoli works great)*. Drizzle with 1 T. lemon juice and 1 T. olive oil. Sprinkle with ½ tsp. salt and ¼ tsp. each pepper, garlic salt, and seasoned salt. Sprinkle 3 T. grated Parmesan cheese over the top. Wrap foil around broccoli to make one tent pack. Cook as directed until broccoli is crisp-tender. **Serves 4**

To grill, place foil pack on the grate over indirect medium heat and cover grill. Cook about 15 minutes.

At the campfire, set foil pack on a few hot coals surrounded by more heat. Cook about 15 minutes, rotating pack once.

Cowboy Packs

For each foil pack meal, layer 1 onion slice, 4 bacon strip halves, about ¼ C. baked beans, and 1 tsp. brown sugar on a large piece of foil. Set a thin hamburger patty on top and sprinkle with seasoned salt. Place a small chunk of fresh sweet corn on the meat and top with some butter and pepper. Wrap foil around the food to make a tent pack. Cook as directed until meat is done and corn is tender. **Each pack serves 1**

To grill, set foil pack(s) on the grate over medium heat and cover grill. Cook 25 to 30 minutes.

At the campfire, set foil pack(s) on medium coals and cook 25 to 30 minutes, rotating twice.

Kielbasa Combo

1 (14 oz.) pkg. kielbasa
   sausage

½ large onion

1 (15 oz.) can whole kernel
   corn, drained

1 (14.5 oz.) can green
   beans, drained

1 tsp. seasoned salt

½ tsp. garlic powder

2 T. butter, softened

Directions

Slice the sausage lengthwise and cut into 1" pieces; place in a large bowl. Slice the onion into rings and add to bowl. Add the corn, green beans, and seasonings; mix well. Divide mixture among five large pieces of foil. Add some of the butter to each pack and fold packs tent-style. Cook as directed. **Serves 5**

Cooking Methods

Set foil packs on the grate over medium heat and cover grill. Cook 15 to 20 minutes or until everything is hot.

Set foil packs on hot coals and cook about 20 minutes or until everything is hot. Rotate packs once or twice during cooking.

For extra zing, use Cajun or Creole seasoning to flavor these packs.

Tilapia & Veggies

4 tilapia fillets,
   thawed if frozen

¼ C. mayonnaise

¼ C. grated Parmesan
   cheese

Salt, paprika, cayenne &
   black pepper to taste

1 zucchini, sliced

2 carrots, peeled & cut
   into matchsticks

½ red bell pepper,
   thinly sliced

1 (12 oz.) pkg. frozen snap
   peas, partially thawed

Directions

Place each fillet on a large piece of sprayed foil; spread mayonnaise evenly over fillets. Sprinkle with cheese and all seasonings. Arrange zucchini, carrots, bell pepper, and snap peas over and around fish. Wrap foil around food to make four tent packs. Cook as directed. **Serves 4**

Cooking Methods

Set foil packs on the grate over medium-high heat and cover grill. Cook 10 to 15 minutes or until fish flakes easily with a fork and vegetables are crisp-tender.

Set foil packs on a few hot coals surrounded by more heat. Cook 10 to 15 minutes, rotating packs partway through cooking time, until fish flakes easily with a fork and vegetables are crisp-tender.

In combo packs like these, cut the vegetables so they'll all finish cooking in the same amount of time.

Jerked Shrimp Tacos

5 C. shredded cabbage

5 T. mayonnaise

1½ T. minced onion

Zest & juice of 1 lime

1 lb. frozen raw shrimp, thawed & peeled

¼ C. butter, melted

2½ to 3 tsp. jerk seasoning *(recipe on next page or purchased)*

Pinch of red pepper flakes

Salt to taste

Chopped fresh parsley

8 corn tortillas

Fresh cilantro

Directions

In a bowl, stir together cabbage, mayonnaise, onion, and lime zest and juice. Cover and chill until needed.

Place shrimp in another bowl with butter, all seasonings, and some parsley; toss until evenly coated. Divide shrimp among two large pieces of doubled, sprayed foil and wrap to make two tent packs. Wrap tortillas in another piece of foil. Cook as directed and serve cabbage mixture and shrimp in the warm tortillas; garnish with cilantro. **Makes 8 tacos**

Cooking Methods

Set shrimp foil packs on the grate over medium-high heat and cover grill. Cook 8 to 10 minutes or until shrimp are pink and fully cooked. Set tortilla foil pack over indirect medium heat until warm, about 5 minutes.

Set shrimp foil packs on medium coals and cook 8 to 10 minutes or until shrimp are pink and fully cooked. Rotate packs and flip over halfway through cooking time. Set tortilla foil pack next to coals until warm.

Jerk Seasoning

Mix 1 T. dried minced onion, 1¼ tsp. dried thyme, 1 tsp. each ground allspice, garlic powder, and pepper, ½ tsp. each cayenne pepper and paprika, and ¼ tsp. each ground cinnamon and salt. Store in an airtight container and use the amount needed in recipes.

SPICY

Lemon Chicken

Set 1 whole chicken on a large double thickness of sprayed foil. Brush with ¼ C. melted butter. Squeeze the juice from 1 lemon over the chicken and sprinkle with lemon pepper, salt, pepper, and paprika. Place ½ sliced onion and remaining lemon peel and pulp inside the chicken. Set sage leaves on top and wrap tightly in foil. Cook as directed until the internal temperature of thigh meat reaches 165°. Let rest 5 minutes before slicing. **Serves 4**

To grill, set foil pack on the grate over indirect medium heat and cook 50 to 60 minutes. Rotate pack several times.

At the campfire, set foil pack on a few hot coals surrounded by more heat. Cook about 1 hour, rotating often. For the last 10 minutes, set hot coals on top of pack to promote browning.

Spicy Sweet Potatoes

Peel and cube 2 lbs. sweet potatoes. In a large skillet, cook 4 chopped bacon strips until almost crisp; pour off grease, leaving bacon in skillet. Add ½ C. sliced onion; sauté until tender. Whisk in ¼ C. jalapeño jelly and 2 T. apple cider vinegar and simmer until smooth; season with salt and pepper. Stir in sweet potatoes until coated. Pour potato mixture onto a large double layer of sprayed foil and wrap to make one tent pack. Cook as directed until potatoes are tender. Top with cilantro, jalapeños, green onion, and lime juice before serving. **Serves 6-8**

To grill, set foil pack on the grate over medium-high heat and cover grill. Cook 20 to 25 minutes.

At the campfire, set foil pack on hot coals and cook 25 to 30 minutes, rotating pack twice.

Cherry-Coconut Crisp

½ C. quick-cooking oats

⅓ C. raw chip or shredded coconut

¼ C. chopped pecans or walnuts

3 T. sugar, divided

½ tsp. ground cinnamon, or more to taste

1½ T. canola oil

1½ T. pure maple syrup

1 (12 oz.) pkg. frozen dark sweet cherries, thawed

1 T. lemon juice

1 T. cornstarch

4 canned pineapple slices, drained

Chocolate chips, optional

Directions

In a small bowl, combine oats, coconut, pecans, 2 tablespoons sugar, and cinnamon. Stir in oil and syrup and set aside.

In a large bowl, combine cherries, remaining 1 tablespoon sugar, lemon juice, and cornstarch; toss well. Place one pineapple slice on each of four pieces of sprayed foil. Spoon cherry mixture evenly over pineapple and top each with part of the oat mixture. Sprinkle with a few chocolate chips, if desired. Wrap foil around food to make four tent packs and cook as directed. **Serves 4**

Cooking Methods

Set foil packs on the grate over medium heat and cook 12 to 14 minutes or until hot.

Set foil packs on medium coals and cook 12 to 16 minutes or until hot, rotating packs once.

Beef Stew Packs

2 lbs. beef chuck roast, fat trimmed

5 or 6 potatoes, peeled & diced

6 carrots, peeled & sliced in rounds

1 (8 oz.) pkg. fresh mushrooms, sliced

⅔ C. chopped onion

2 celery ribs, sliced

2 (10.5 oz.) cans golden mushroom soup

Chopped fresh parsley

Salt & pepper to taste

Hot pepper sauce, optional

6 ice cubes

Directions

Grease six large double thicknesses of foil with cooking spray. Cut the roast into small cubes. Divide roast, potatoes, carrots, mushrooms, onion, and celery evenly among foil pieces. Spoon about ⅓ can soup over each serving. Sprinkle with parsley, salt, and pepper; add a few drops of hot pepper sauce, if desired. Place one ice cube on each serving and wrap foil around food to make six tent packs. Cook as directed. **Serves 6**

Cooking Methods

 Set foil packs on the grate over medium-low heat and cover grill. Cook 50 to 60 minutes or until beef and vegetables are tender.

 Set foil packs on medium coals and cook 50 to 60 minutes or until beef and vegetables are tender. Rotate packs several times during cooking.

Dry Rub Seasoning

Stir together 1 T. each brown sugar, paprika, and chili powder, 1 tsp. each garlic powder and salt, and black pepper to taste. This makes enough dry rub to generously coat 2 to 3 lbs. of ribs or other cuts of beef.

SPICY

BBQ Short Ribs

2 lbs. boneless beef
  short ribs

Dry rub seasoning *(recipe
on previous page or
purchased)*

8 ice cubes

Barbecue sauce

Directions

Generously coat the ribs with dry rub seasoning and place in a covered dish. Chill about 1 hour.

To cook, grease four double thicknesses of foil. Arrange two or three ribs on each foil piece along with two ice cubes. Wrap foil around meat to make four tent packs. Cook as directed and serve with barbeque sauce. **Serves 4-6**

Cooking Methods

Set foil packs on the grate over indirect medium heat and cover grill. Cook 1½ to 2 hours or until tender. If desired, fold foil back and brush meat with barbeque sauce; cover grill and cook 5 minutes more.

Set foil packs on a few hot coals surrounded by more heat. Cook 1½ to 2 hours or until tender, rotating packs and flipping over several times during cooking. If desired, open packs and brush meat with barbeque sauce; reseal foil and cook 5 to 10 minutes more.

Check meat several times to be sure packs retain moisture. Add water or more ice cubes, if necessary.

Thanksgiving Dinner

For each dinner, place 1 turkey cutlet *(⅓ to ½ lb.)* on a large double thickness of sprayed foil. Top with 1 C. prepared stuffing and arrange ½ C. frozen *(thawed)* green beans around turkey. Pour ½ C. turkey gravy over everything and sprinkle with ¼ C. dried sweetened cranberries. Season with salt, pepper, dried thyme, and dried marjoram. Wrap foil around food in a tent pack and cook as directed until turkey is done *(internal temperature should reach 165°)*. **Each pack serves 1**

To grill, set foil pack(s) on the grate over medium heat and cover grill. Cook about 20 minutes.

At the campfire, set foil pack(s) on medium coals surrounded by more heat. Cook about 20 minutes, rotating once.

Pumpkin Muffins

Cut 8 large oranges in half and scoop out the flesh to make
16 shells. In a bowl, mix 1 (14 oz.) pkg. Pumpkin Quick Bread &
Muffin Mix with water, oil, and eggs as directed on the package.
Fill each orange shell halfway with batter *(you may have extra)*.
Wrap shells individually in sprayed foil to make 16 tent packs
and cook as directed until muffins test done with a toothpick.
Makes 16 muffins

To grill, set foil packs on the grate over medium heat
(batter side up) and cover grill. Cook 10 to 15 minutes.

At the campfire, set foil packs on hot coals surrounded
by more heat *(be sure they set level with batter side up)*. Cook
10 to 15 minutes.

Index